OUR GOD COMES

OUR GOD COMES

And Will Not Be Silent

Marlene Chase

Crest ✠ Books
Salvation Army National Publications
Alexandria, Virginia

© 2000 The Salvation Army

Published by Crest Books, Salvation Army National Publications
615 Slaters Lane, Alexandria, Virginia 22314
(703) 684-5500 Fax: (703) 684-5539
www.salvationarmyusa.org

Printed in the United States of America

All rights reserved. No part of this publication may be reproduced, stored in a retrieval system, or transmitted in any form or by any means—electronic, mechanical, photocopy, recording—without the prior written permission of the publisher. The only exception is brief quotations in printed reviews.

Unless otherwise noted, Scripture taken from the *Holy Bible, New International Version*. Copyright 1973, 1978, 1984 by International Bible Society. Used by permission. All rights reserved.

Cover and book design by Kristin B. Griffin

Photographs in text by Diane Tolcher (with the exception of the image on pg. 12)

Library of Congress Catalog Card Number: 00–110769

ISBN: 0–9704870–0–2

To Howard, Evangeline and Laurel—
  my heart's best treasures.

Contents

INTRODUCTION	1

I. OUR GOD COMES IN THE GLORY OF CREATION AND COMMUNITY

Promise	4
October Again!	4
The Necklace	5
Daddy's Visit	5
Jenny	6
Royal Treasures	7
Nexus	8
Lady November	9
Quest	9
To an Abused Child	10
The Door	10
Cry the Beloved Children	11
His Immeasurable Self	13
Moses Revisited	13
November	14
Solzhenitsyn's Trees	15
Practical Joke	16
An Old One in the House	16
First Snowfall	17
Of Wendy, Dying of Cancer	18
The Staircase	19
Prayer in Winter	20
His Comfort	20
Valentine Reverie	21
God's Economy	21
The Birthing	22
Discovery	22
Fanfare	23
Magnanimous Spring	23
Little Baptists	24
Messenger	25

April's Gone	25
The Trump Card	26
Memorial Day Weekend	26
Perspective	27
Firefly Day	27
I Saw God	28
Morning Gift	28
July the Fourth	30
Mantis	31
Savor Summer Days	32
Morning Song	33
Farewell to Summer	33
What's in a Birthday?	34
Prayer for Passing Time	34
When You Have to Say Goodbye	35

II. OUR GOD COMES IN TRANSFORMING LOVE

Three–fold Praise to Christ Our Lord	38
I. The Cosmic Christ	38
II. The Incarnate Christ	39
III. The Triumphant King	40
On Second Thought	41
Child's Play	42
Epiphany	43
Grace	43
Gift for Baby	44
Good Friday Prayer	45
In Search of Self	46
Have I the Right?	46
Sin	48
Lily of the Valley	48
Mary's Moment	49
One Christmas More	50
New Baby in the House	51
Holiday Hunger	51
Remedy	52

The Silence of the Lamb	52
Supply and Demand	53
Scavenger	54
The Gift Exchange	54
Transfigured	55
When All the Candles Are Gone Away	56
Alive in Christ	57
The Trade	58
Peter's Epiphany	59

III. OUR GOD COMES IN THE FELLOWSHIP OF HIS SPIRIT

From Crisis to Cure	62
After the Rain	62
Anorexia	63
Breathing Lessons	64
The Spirit and the Church	65
Bold Reticence	65
Confession	66
The Source	66
My Life is a Poem	68
Laodicean Lament	69
Intrusion	69
Hospitality	70
Oblation	70
Proximity	71
Consummation	71
Winter Meditation	72
Word Choice	72
A Prayer in Wait	74
Arpeggio	75
Punakaiki Pun	76
Math Problem	78

Acknowledgments

The author thanks the following publications, in whose pages certain of these poems first appeared.

Magazines:

At Ease, The Banner, Channels, Christian Herald, Discoveries, Evangel, Herald of Holiness, Living Streams, The Muse, The Officer, On the Line, Pentecost Evangel, Silver Wings, Standard, Time of Singing, Today's Man, The War Cry.

Books:

A Seed in the Wind (The Salvation Army Central Territory, 1991)
Christmas Through the Years (Crest Books, 1998)
Pictures From the Word (Crest Books 1998)
Easter Through the Years (Crest Books, 1999)

Introduction

A Psalm addressed to Asaph, one of David's three choir leaders, begins with this perennially present promise: "Our God comes and will not be silent" (50:3). Life is a quest to distinguish His voice ... in the silence of our childhood when a thousand voices call to us, but none more clearly than the voice of Him who so recently fashioned us. Our Lord comes in the silence of our adolescence when our passions and probing pull us in many directions, but none strong enough to stifle the yearning that propels us upward. Our God comes in adulthood when achievements and accolades accumulate but do not satisfy. We bend yet nearer toward the One voice that alone makes sense of who we are and long to be.

The poet in us all hears Him in the roar of thunder and the rustle of wind. We see Him in the desert flower and the lightning bug, in the silent tumble of a crimson leaf and the cataclysmic surge of sea. In every subtle nuance or cyclonic clash of nature "Our God comes and will not be silent." He comes in the eye and voice of child and parent, neighbor and lover. And when these pictures were blurred or distorted, He sent one clear image of Himself to be swaddled in earth's poor rags and suckled at a human breast. Three decades and more He walked as one of us, but not *quite* one of us, for never was His perfection, His magnificence, distorted. And when He had to leave us, paradox of paradoxes, He never left at all. Our God comes in the person of His indwelling Spirit.

This small volume is divided to speak of His coming in nature and community, through the Incarnation and in the coming of the Holy Spirit whose ongoing work in our lives testifies "Our God comes and will not be silent." He comes! It is but the ear that is deaf, the ear of the soul deadened by repeated blows sustained in our sin—bent world. Each of us could speak of the unique embrace of our God who comes, but the privilege is mine in this small book. In the pages and poems that follow I share my own journey, the sights and sounds, the sensations and visions that witness to the Psalmist's affirmation, "Our God Comes." May He come to you in some new insight, some reborn memory, and speak as only our God can speak.

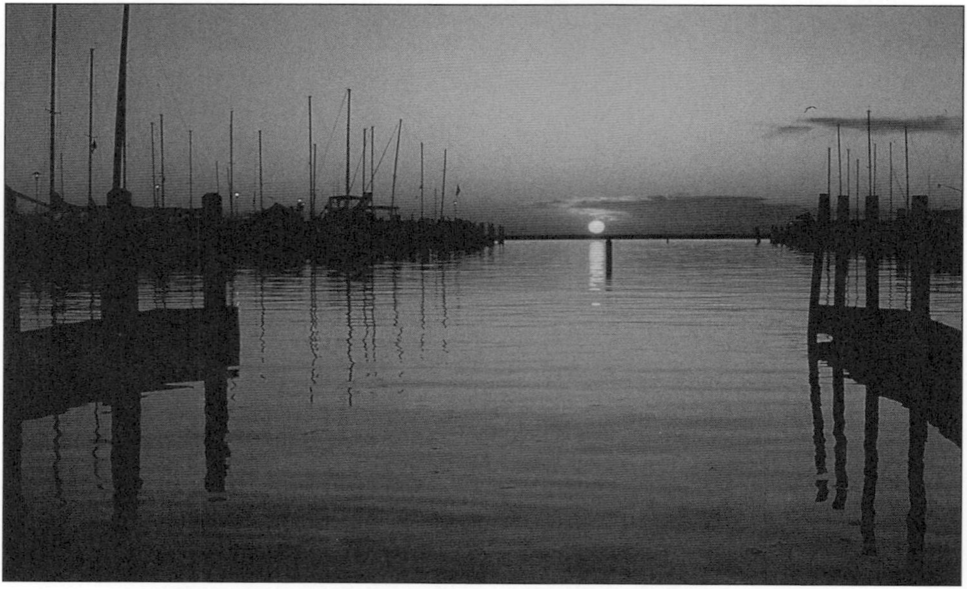

Our God Comes in the Glory of Creation and Community

Poised above the constellations, planets pirouette at His feet and stars stream from His fingertips. From His lips the four winds swirl the heavens, rush down mountain peaks, churn ocean waves that roll and roar and crash to the music of His great soul. To this magnificence our triune God added His highest creation ... and man became a living soul to serve God in community and to enjoy Him forever.

Promise
"Our God comes and will not be silent" (Psalm 50:3).

He comes ... in the thundering tumble of wind
down a greening hill
when all the world is wrapped in Him.
He comes in a ballerina dance
of chartreuse and rosy silk—
virginal visage of beauty
lingering on the mind, promising
something you cannot forget.
He comes to the wintering ground—
ravished, silent, spent—
and wakens it to joy.
In everything He whispers, thunders,
comforts, weeps, and laughs.
"Our God comes and will not be silent."

October Again!

When days dwindle and fires rise,
skies welcome peans of maple praise
braised in molten orange and gold.
Hold these days in fierce embrace;
grace are they, God's burning love.

THE NECKLACE

Circles of time—invisible links
in a great silver chain.
Like a charm I'm suspended
from one small loop.
What holds my fragile link
in place—and what place
is this? This time in which
I dangle and shine and dance,
one of numberless links
all hung together on
a single inscrutable clasp
circling the breast of God?

DADDY'S VISIT

He swept into my room on the weeping winter wind.
Night frost glazed his cheeks, shimmered in his eyes.
Silent, lest he leave, I lay inert and trembling
when at last his breath came spinning
with sweet–sour wine and whispers,
with songs too sad for singing,
with promises unpromised.
He drew a furry treasure from the pocket of his coat
and tucked it warm beside me in the cradle of my arms.
He touched me with his eyes, then vanished into night.
I hugged the little kitten—hugged it 'til it cried.
And I cried with childish passion
and longed for him instead.

JENNY

Fourteen, lost, and going nowhere.
Cold eyes, glacier blue,
one eyebrow sculptured.
Part of her auburn hair is
shaved, oddly eccentric.
She speaks in four–letter words
with a bawdy brashness, bitter
as unripe apples plucked
too soon ... torn ... plundered.
"I'll be dead by eighteen," she says.
Better to contemplate death
than the terror of living
or the living death of boredom.
She stares an icy rebuke,
fuelled by an inward fear.
"Come to the fire," I say,
"a loving heart's fire" ...
but she fears the fire that burns
like ice on a warm tongue.
"Get away from me," she says
while her eyes beg you to stay.
Oh, God of the fourteen and lost,
what cost to redeem a fettered soul!
Blood as red as her hair, her lips,
as red and deep as Calvary Love!

Royal Treasures

Fire blazing on the hill,
embers lining clouds
crimson, silver, gold—
God's treasures counted,
extravagantly spilled.
He could have chosen
to recall His fiery star
in discreet silence.
Instead He gifts the world
with nightly sunsets, feasts
for famished souls.
We go on our way refreshed,
reminded we are kings
and queens and richly loved—
oh, so richly loved!

Nexus

We stand in separate woods.
But once in a long ago we bloomed
in one lemon–green glade,
limbs entwining, growing strong.
Ours were the pale patches of sun,
the ribald poetry of rain.
We greeted sunlit dawns and twilight shades
through all our yearning years.

Then came the quick uprooting,
the tearing and replanting.

Thriving in our separate woods
with mottled memories for shade,
October settles softly down.
Winds sing solitary songs,
disturbing, unleafing us.

It's lonely in my separate wood.
And winter lingers long and cold.
But can it be that sudden leaf,
carried on the windward years,
has only just been torn away,
my brother, from the heart of you?

Lady November

Full–figured and fine,
she begins her slow undressing.
She's turned all but the last lamp down
and sheds each fragrant garment
with slow and measured grace.
She drops her crimson cape
and folds it soft away.
Down flows the fine fur drape,
the gown of green and gold.
She hesitates in the gathering gloom,
shivers, hugs herself
with supple brown arms.
A tear escapes; she reaches
for the last glowing lamp
and night
descends

Quest

In tender tandem with the night,
I make my silent search
by starshine and the moon's white light—
quietly as in a church—
to anthem of windblown leaves
singing in the grass.
Crickets bow their noisy knees
and piously they pass.

To an Abused Child

What can we say to you, dear child,
so fresh from heaven's womb?
You are bruised for our iniquities,
wounded for our transgressions.

Who will declare your generation
who only came to love us?
For you are cut off from the land of the living,
stricken, smitten, afflicted.

Can we hide from you our faces,
despise, reject you still,
much as we did another Child
who came in love to heal?

The Door

The living watch the dying,
wondering what they see.
What music penetrates
those silent barricades
where you cannot enter?
It's hard to sleep
when someone's at the door.
Perhaps he'll step through it
when you are unaware
and there will be no calling back.
You're left with silence
and the swinging door.

Cry the Beloved Children

Oh, the pain of the world's children!
Oh, the children of the world's pain!
Who can comfort us but You,
Oh, Child of God and God of children?

Lead us through the mine fields
with hands held fast in Yours.
Does our clinging hurt You?
Incite the old wounds
wicked hammers left behind?
Does salt from sweaty palms
make You wince or cry?
Are You vulnerable still

To the pain of the world's children,
to the children of the world's pain?
Who can comfort us but You,
Oh, Child of God and God of children?

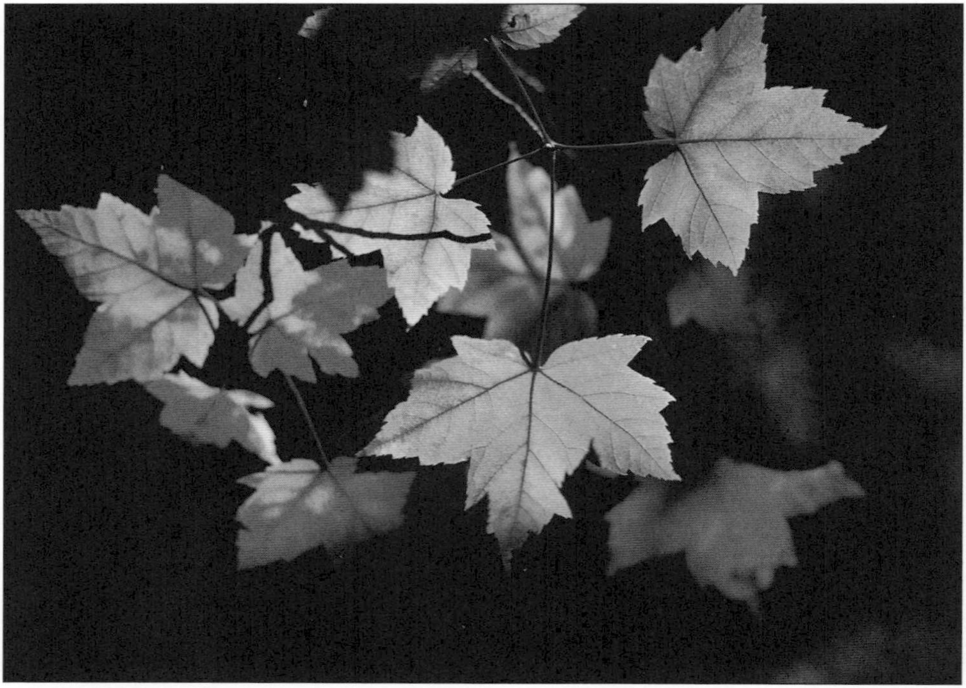

His Immeasurable Self

One tree of flaming symmetry
burns in the autumn sky.
It halts us! We're undone!
One leaf gives way to more,
crimson, saffron, silver, brown.
Our hearts break for beauty.
If what He's made so overwhelms,
how will it be when He
breaks through the eastern sky?
We could die of His immeasurable self!

Moses Revisited

He speaks in a flaming autumn tree,
burning but unconsumed.
My stricken heart unroomed
trembles at the bold decree,
"This is holy ground!"

November

Sweet stillness of gray November.
Leaves, like trailing glory clouds,
settle, stir, die and bury
to wait a slow rebirth. We live in
November—this poor dying time,
but April comes, inexorable, sudden,
when we shall live more nobly and well.
Still, this lingering is sweet.
Precious the gray November
and every memory of April past,
every thought of April to come.
Precious—for every moment in life and death
God is awake.

Solzhenitsyn's Trees

Goodness, Truth, Beauty—
arbored trinity—
growing tall,
embracing all.

A careless world won't wait
but rushes to amputate
Truth and Good,
as firewood!

But Beauty's noble lure
whimsical, pure
may alone stand
contraband.

Upon reading Solzhenitsyn's Nobel Prize Lecture

Practical Joke

Summer in November—
lingering, and mild,
but we are not beguiled.
Our hearts remember
winter waits in the wings,
costumed and practiced,
ready to perform.

Soon will fall the curtain,
bold he'll make his entry.
No more the silent sentry,
his role is cast and certain.

An Old One in the House

An old one in the house
helps us live more fully,
reminding us of the living past,
the fleeting present
and the eternal future.
He helps us live in each
with gratitude and love,
realizing all there is to savor
or to lose.

First Snowfall

Heaven's vigorous sieve opens
and spills its crystal contents.
In a few white hours of grace,
the world slows down,
holds its tongue,
and we reach out our own
to catch the stinging drops.
Its icy power stops us
in our languid steps,
compels us to be clean—
as pure as these flakes
covering our dark sins.
Call for the signature Artist!
Call Him in. Plead for Him to
paint this white, white world
inside our hearts!

Of Wendy, Dying of Cancer

Can she feel it creeping,
sneaking, stealing
one cell after another
in the descending dark?

Could God stand by
and watch this suffering
without getting inside
the agony Himself?

She is not alone.
He too has beckoned pain,
faced the long, dark march
single–file,
eyes to the lambent light.

THE STAIRCASE
Song of Solomon 8:6

The sad watch has begun.
It has been dusk for days.
Surely now the curtain
will fall, the hard sweet release.
But no, light still filters in,
hovers as they watch and wait
with tears unshed
sins unpardoned,
meanings mistaken,
endings unended.

If there are steps to death,
do they descend or wind upward?
Do we linger midway—
go up or down
or play at passing?
It is a hard thing, hard as love.
At the bottom of the staircase,
turn, turn, ascend
and see it has no end.
"Love is as strong as death."

Prayer in Winter

Lord, I was too frustrated to notice the beauty of the gift you sent today. I was weary of sloshing about, hampered by the thick, white stuff ... I didn't notice how it shone in the catch of sunlight, how it clung thick and white to yearning tree fingers. I didn't think to thank You for the purity, the serenity of it embracing earth's heart. I only thought how dreary to hunt for boots in a closet full of junk, how tedious to steer my car through icy winter streets. I mumbled through the trying day, until suddenly I stopped to really look.

How sad, the day ends with the last gleam of sunlight on crystal, and I missed the pleasure of this day's gift from Your hand. Let there be another snow, Lord, as artfully lovely as this one, as full of diamonds and magic as this one. Let there be another, and I shall not waste it. But I wonder—what else have I missed, Lord, with these eyes that do not see?

His Comfort

It falls—a solitary tear—
and lodges comfortless,
cold, caught
between heart and soul.
One knows, sees it shimmer,
but does not reach
to wipe it away
or hurry it.
But one of His own
slides silently toward it,
covers, glistens
like sun on morning dew.
They wait as one
for surcease.

Valentine Reverie

I watch two logs side by side
in the dying winter night.
Sharing one flame they settle close
and burn with one sweet light.
I hear them whisper, gauging time
lest one should burn more strong.
Then in the dim, dancing dark
they burst as one in song.
Two logs, like our two hearts,
burn with luminescent flame.
Each crackling ember in unison
beats with the other's name.

God's Economy
Psalm 56:8

He saved my tears in His bottle
for some purpose too grand to waste.
I had thought tears useless—
unpleasant to taste.
But He has planned another Cana
turned water into wine,
to make of want abundance,
of sorrow joy.

The Birthing

Premature spring—
skies robin's egg blue
incubating in the sun.
Branches quiver like
a green umbilical.
A fertile womb
counts each contraction
ready to bear down
and release its young.

Discovery

"He loves me, He loves me not ..."
It was always a guessing game.
Sometimes yes, sometimes no,
but seldom twice the same.

God sent His holy Flower
born of love's free will,
and every falling petal speaks,
"He loves me, He loves me still."

Fanfare

A sunbeam found the tatter
in my early turned—down shade
and broke upon my bleakness
like a new—born star's parade.

I heard the marching music
of a lone triumphant flute
and, swallowing the rising ache,
I stood in the silence, mute.

Magnanimous Spring

In spite of our winter souls,
Spring has come
with smiles and open arms.
She laughs at our confessions,
demanding no penance
but acceptance
of her green gifts tied
with pastel ribbons
and strewn at our feet.

Little Baptists

Since first light they've been alert to the world,
filling it with their feathered machinations ...
Nest building, practice flies from eave to branch—
warnings, announcements—heady stuff.
Pecking and fluttering, gathering and stashing,
feathering, twittering, chattering, singing
bird lullabies for their yearning young
soon to settle beneath their wings,
to incubate in explosive silence.
But now the roof is a charged mad scene!
Time to work—so much to do—
so much to crow about!
Like little Baptists they flurry.
Prepare! Prepare! Make way
for what is soon to come!

Should not we all be forerunners,
charging the world like these busy ones?
This is the time for building,
warning, work and practiced praise
as we watch with ever vigilant eye
the eastern skies.

Messenger

Warble on, sweet warbler
beneath my early window.
You warm my withered spirit
and wing heaven near.

In our world so full of words
not worthy to be said,
yours that cannot be defined
bring order that sustains.

April's Gone

In a blaze of May,
her subtlety diffused
with grandiose display.
We didn't cherish her when
she wept so quietly,
danced so lightly then
across the stage of spring ...
a chartreuse ballerina
swept on gossamer wing.

The Trump Card

April, said Eliot, is the cruelest month,
dealing snow to daffodil cups
and frost glaze on strawberry fields.
Citrus will cost more now—
such a penny ante, compared
with a single cardinal's flame,
a purple crocus cracking clay.
April's tricks hardly fool God
(Master of the universe He),
who plays the trump card every time!

Memorial Day Weekend

I'm waving good-bye again,
loitering on the lawn as you
dangle car keys in your hand.
We can't quite end this day—
there's so much yet to say.
Your other world calls
and you must answer.
I'm loathe to let you go,
to catch that final wave.
Will you come again
or must I be content
with remembering,
Decembering in May?

PERSPECTIVE

From my hotel window
buildings dwarf
the misty Colorado mountains.
Skyscrapers tower
above the subtle peaks.
How small God's handiwork!
How immense the work of man!
Or is it my perspective?

Couched in this commercial valley,
too close to comprehend,
have I placed a fist before my eyes
and blotted out the sun?

FIREFLY DAY

Another day has flashed past
with the brief brilliance
of a firefly on a summer night.
A small spark in so great a black sky.
Does it delight because it is
so vulnerable, so transient?
Capture the spark in mid–flight!
Capture it if you can but
do not weep that it refuses
to shine until
released once more.

I Saw God
For my Grandchildren

I saw God today
in a rainbow arching high
across the sky.
I heard God whisper love
in a sweeping summer breeze
waking up leaves.

I felt God's touch today
in the soft cuddle of kittens
like wooly mittens.
In rainbows and kittens and wind,
in all created things,
His love sings!

Morning Gift

God moves through shadowed woods,
turning on lights at His pleasure.
Unlocking His house of hallowed goods,
He smiles as He counts His treasure.
Then in one lavish, golden day
He gives them all away.

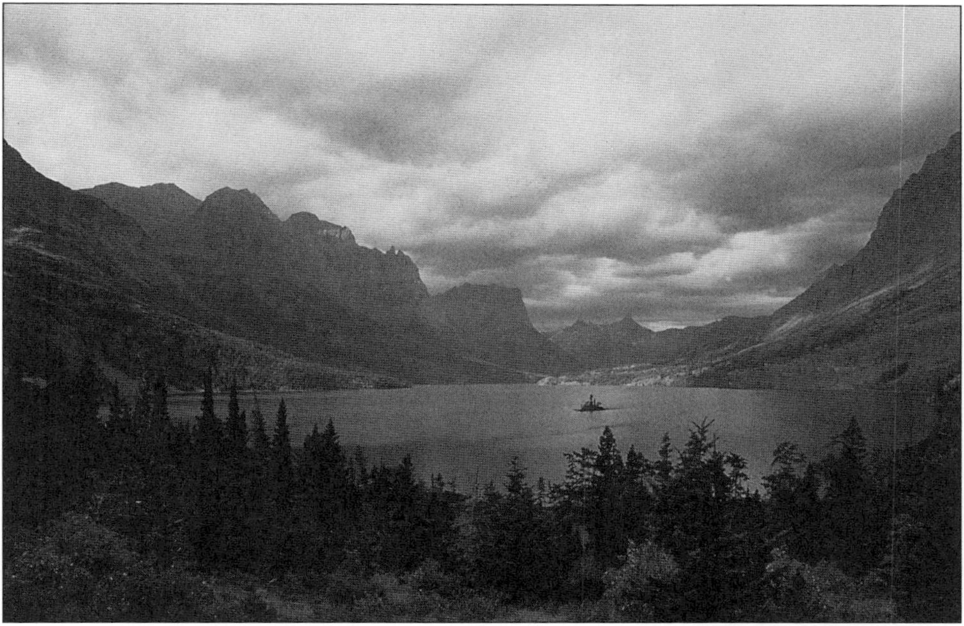

July the Fourth

Celebrate freedom
with bursts of color and fire
high above confining roofs
and summer–filled eaves.

Cry freedom
with rolling thunder under–
scoring our routine lives
and our dazzling dreams.

Cherish freedom,
its glory, pain and honor,
its sorrow and dearly bought joy—
all its blood–red legacies.

Pray freedom
shall not end or fade away
like sparklers on summer lawns,
aborted fizzles on porches.

Hold freedom
in hallowed hearts and minds,
in the center of our souls
where it is most costly to be free.

Mantis

I flushed it out this morning
with my careless garden hose.
Rose the lithe, green body,
fragile feelers pawing,
clawing cold chrysanthemums.
It straddled tender stems
as waters quickly flooded.
Hooded eyes closed,
it made its insect prayer.

I too hear the lurching,
surging flood below
and rise, straining,
my whole green self
gasping for God.

Savor Summer Days

Languid days, long and mellow—
lawns and lemonade, yellow
and sweet and soothing.
Fresh cut grass and roses,
children dancing in garden hoses
and the old ones talking soft and low.
A song from a convertible's radio
drones in the heavy air, and things
we loved seem close and right
and lightning bugs on lawns at night
bring the child in us racing back.
Pack up winter and tuck it away.
Savor life these golden summer days.

Morning Song

The raucous caw of crows
pierce the quiet wood—
primeval, thieves all,
scavengers of dying and dead.
Mourning doves moan the dirge
from grim sideline pews.
And just when I am grieved,
bereaved of all but dread,
one clear trill of the lark
sanctifies the day!

Farewell to Summer

Gently she lingers,
deep summer unwilling
to fall soft away.
Clasps now his fingers,
her golden sun spilling
a final love ray.

What's in a Birthday?

A thousand little moments
cluster in a birthday
like stones in a cherished ring ...
The shining moments you have lived
and loved and smiled and hurt.
In each God's grace has been the setting,
strong, engraved, secure.

Prayer for Passing Time

I vowed to spend less time
mourning the moments past
than welcoming those in wait,
but still the sadness tugs
as summer falls away
and I weep for time gone by.
Let me laugh as days draw nigh
and love each one unerringly.

When You Have to Say Goodbye

When you have to say goodbye
say it with gratitude for moments
and memories that linger after
the hushed farewell is spoken.

Say it with prayer, holding
each other in the hallowed place
where nothing is wasted, nothing is lost,
not even the falling tear.

Say it with heart, recalling
"a day is as a thousand years
and a thousand years but a day"
in the economy of grace.

Say it with faith, giving
God the keeping of your love,
the fulfillment of your tender trust
in His inscrutable plan.

Say it with hope knowing
you'll one day say hello again
if only in the inviolate heart
that keeps its treasures well.

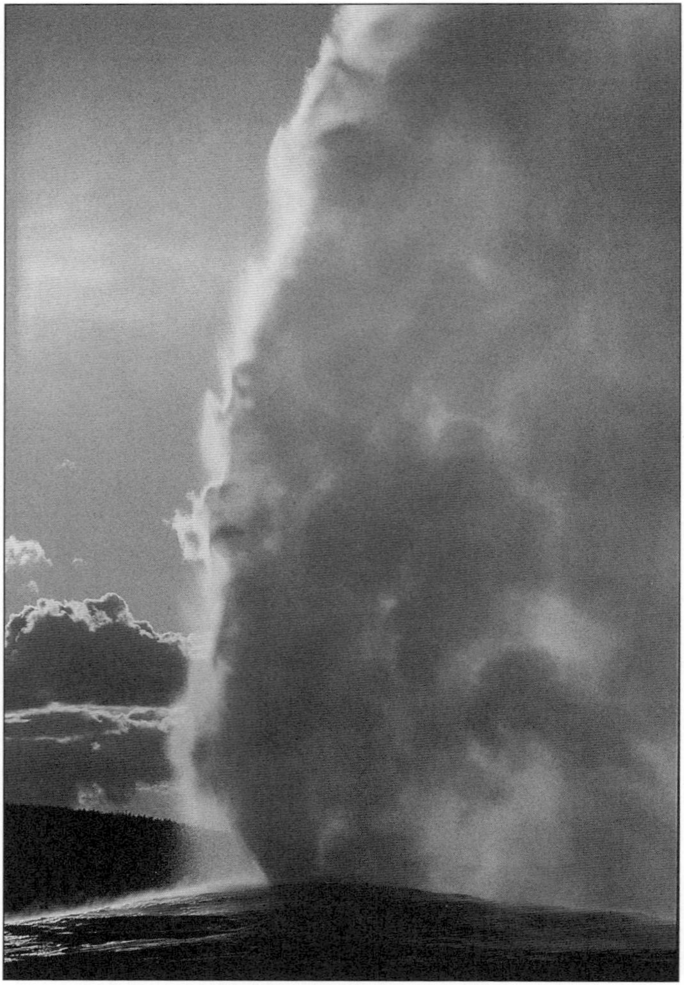

Our God Comes in Transforming Love

Just before a flaming maple leaf fell away from a blackened bough, we caught a glimpse of God. When the seas thundered and broke upon the shore, we held our breath in wonder of their Creator. We hovered in the shadow of the mighty mountain where His garments were mystery, His face a forbidding sun, His mind unattainable as constellations, His heart—ah, His great heart! To know it, to feel its beating—unthinkable!

And suddenly, when the gulf between us widened impenetrable and deep, and blackness swirled about us, a star appeared in the eastern sky. A tiny cry echoed over the distant hills of Judea. "The people walking in darkness have seen a great light ... Call His name Jesus, for He will save His people from their sins" (Matt. 1:21).

He comes to show us the way back to God, to the glory of His friendship. He comes to transform our darkness into His glorious light. "Lo, He comes with healing in His wings."

Three-Fold Praise to Christ Our Lord

Christ is the image of the invisible God, the firstborn over all creation. For by Him all things were created, things in heaven and on earth, visible and invisible, whether thrones or powers or rulers or authorities; all things were created by Him and for Him. He is before all things, and in Him all things hold together. And He is the head of the body, the church; He is the beginning and the firstborn from among the dead, so that in everything He might have the supremacy. For God was pleased to have all His fullness dwell in Him, and through Him to reconcile to Himself all things, whether things on earth or things in heaven, by making peace through His blood, shed on the cross (Col. 1:15–20).

I. The Cosmic Christ

Poised above the constellations,
planets pirouette at His feet and
stars stream from His fingertips.
From His lips the four winds swirl
across the heavens, down mountain peaks,
churning ocean waves that roll and roar
and crash to the music of His great soul.
Green plains, swollen with praise,
burst with goldenrod, purple heather,
jack pine and lily, rhododendron and rose.
Watching with eyes that never sleep,
He cradles His universe child.
Yet some deep yearning
stirs His heart, and man emerges,
released from a resplendent Womb.
A living soul to share His heart!
A mind to know His thoughts!
Heaven erupts in spontaneous joy
to lullaby the children of His love.

II. The Incarnate Christ

The angels bow in ignorant remorse,
their praise mellowed by His pain
as His love children traverse the earth
without an upward glance,
intent on their small subduing
of a world they claim as theirs.
Love compels Him from His throne.
The Creator becomes the created.
Mewling, cooing, flailing infant arms
in which galaxies once danced,
the Holy Babe is suckled at human breasts.
Hands that fashioned stars
now hammer rude planks.
He walks among them, the God–man,
knowing intimately human need,
healing the deaf, the blind, the dead.
Soon enough, holy hands and feet
learn the hammer's rage.
The tree Omnipotence planted holds Him
suspended between earth and heaven.

III. The Triumphant King

Down the years His blood has flowed,
a river wide enough, deep enough
to consume the wild rages of sin.
Beneath its pure waves men have plunged
to find themselves alive as He.
Alive to love that shimmers, dances
and compels their homeward hearts.
Once more He leaves the hearth of heaven
to guide His children home.
This time, no mewling, cooing Babe
but the King emblazoned with glory
and dazzling in holy light.
See Him recall the four winds,
coil the oceans in His robe,
wrap up stars and galaxies in His train.
Fashioned in purity and shining joy,
His Bride rises to meet the Lord!

On Second Thought

I'm not sure I want you to
"make Calvary real to me"—
scourging whips and nails,
curses and the cursed tree.
Stale sweat, clotting blood
and Jesus falling on the road.

Do I really want to hear
the jeering shouts and cries,
see timeless love impaled
and terror in children's eyes?
I cringe as mighty mountains shake—
and Jesus dies for mankind's sake.

But Calvary must be real
as real as sin's deep stain,
and one must take its dread scenes in
if he would rise and live again.

Child's Play

What shall we give this little Child
Who had the mountains for His toys,
Who scooped the valleys up like jacks,
sent them rolling, and bounced the sun
to the pinnacle of sky?
Who intricately carved white flakes
and watched them lace the velvet sky?
Who bent the boughs like boomerangs
and flung them far across the plains?
What bauble shall we give to Him
Who strung the purple drape of night
and draws it back with bands of gold?
Who made the kaleidoscope of stars
and twirled it deftly round and round?
Who splashed His bootless feet in seas
and sailed aloft the ocean waves?
Who carved the mammoth jigsaw world
and joined each continent with ease?
What can we give the King of life?
Give one pure–lit, eternal flame
wrapped up in flesh and bone.

Epiphany

The prophets spoke,
their holy fingers grasping light,
and I trembled in my darkness.

The angels spoke,
their gleaming figures wreathed in light,
and I longed to touch their shining.

Then Jesus spoke,
and light broke through my flesh and bone
and wrapped around my heart.

Grace

Dressed in a shining gown of light,
grace comes singing on the wind.
Its train, translucent in the night,
drapes the ragged bones of sin,
clothes man's primeval pain,
misery's monumental flow.
Grace descends with pure–lit train
and follows where the naked go.

Gift for Baby

He's come, Emmanuel,
newborn Son of the living God.
But starlight traces a shadow
across the holy manger bed,
and sentinel at His feet
waits the gift of myrrh.

The gift of death for God?
What do you mean, foolish wise man
to lay such a gift at His feet?
Gold and noble frankincense
are proper gifts for kings.
Why do you bring Him myrrh?

In Mary's solemn gaze,
wonder and uncertainty
give way to sudden pain
as echoes of the angels' words
come winging on the wind
with essence of bitter myrrh.

Born to die? God,
what terrible joy Your coming brings!
"Call His name Jesus,
for He shall save us from our sins."
We bow in humble worship
and bless the gift of myrrh.

Good Friday Prayer

You wept over Jerusalem
and sweat great drops of blood.
We scarcely notice other souls
until they interrupt our lives.
The Father's will was Your meat,
Your drink, Your vital breath.
But we, Your selfish children, do only
what seems to us good, beneficial,
and when You don't play by our rules,
we take our hearts like hoarded playthings
and stumble wounded home.

Teach us how to weep again
out of righteous hearts that hate
the darkness and savagery of men.
Keep the pain of others in our eyes
like graven stains of indelible ink
mirroring our dead soul's blight
that only blood can wash away.
Keep us in such a place, O Lord,
where those sweaty drops shall fall on us.
Humble our passionate hearts until
they beat as one with Yours.

In Search of Self

Years of malnourishment,
feeding on waxed fruit
from a crystal bowl
drives us, half crazed,
to starvation.

Feasting on solitude
and Self–absorption
we search the far corners
from east to west,
still hungry.

Have I the Right?

Have I the right to call upon You
in my extremity
when I've neglected You
in my opportunity?
Yet You welcome my temerity,
forgive my bold iniquity!

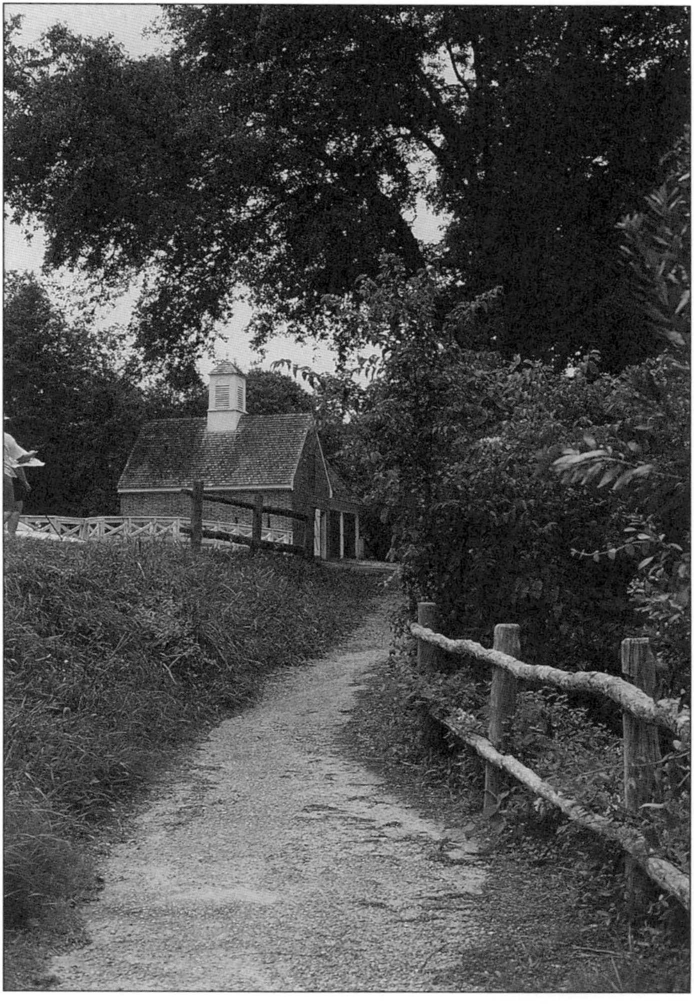

Sin

The worm that bores
in the lush, red rose
steals its sweetness,
riddles its richness.
As Blake knows,
"Oh, rose,
thou art sick."

How does the conquered thing yet live
when its death was devised
by so great a Lover
and Gardener of roses?

Lily of the Valley

I know why they call You "Lily"—
flower of sweetest fragrance
spilled for all who chance
to linger in the valley.

Your pristine sacrifice,
like seeds in the rain,
cleanse the dry world's pain
and grow a Paradise.

Mary's Moment

Crouched in the corner of Simon's house
like a hollow, cast–off urn
holding only the dust of dreams,
she waits.

Something shining in His eyes
wrenches her captive heart.
Why do they offer Him no wine,
no bread?

Tears, born of uncommon love,
fall like rain on His feet,
and her desert of dying dreams
blossoms.

One Christmas More

The star draws near again
to ancient Bethlehem.
And still we seek
though famished, weak
to catch a glimpse of Him
who gives one Christmas more
from time's depleting store.
He calls us down the dwindling year:
"Come and dine, your life is here."

Here in the lowly shed
where dogs and cattle are fed
is the best, the living Bread
fragrant on the hearth.

New Baby in the House

Did she long to entertain them—
the guests who came to call?
Coffee or tea for the Magi?
A seat by the fire for the shepherds?
A sweet for the mythical drummer boy?
Would she have liked new carpet,
ornaments to delight her visitors' eyes?
A well–laid table with silver settings?
She had but straw and a mystical star—
the work of Another's hands.
Christmas was a solitary vigil
for Mary who "pondered all those things,"
not slighted that her guests
had eyes only for the Child of Christmas.

Holiday Hunger

Yearning for magic or love
we make our way to Christmas—
stumbling, blind, swept in a tide
of shopping, dancing, decking
halls instead of hearts.

God seems not to condemn
our mad holiday rush
but waits once more undecorated
in the center of it all
and calls our poor hearts home.

Remedy

Willingly He embraced
our human burden
and all the festering impediments
of our dangerous blood.
It took the holy stream
spilt on Golgotha's hill,
a transfusion in one pure,
unremitting flood,
to heal us
and make us whole.

The Silence of the Lamb

*"As a sheep before her shearers is silent,
so He did not open His mouth" (Isa. 53:7).*

His was no silence of repression,
or of studied pain;
not for sake of impression,
pity or disdain
but a holy silence, not denying
all that love must give—
the shearing, bleeding, dying
that other sheep might live.

Supply and Demand

How crude your manger, Lord,
a feeding trough
from which the beasts ate
until it was empty, dry.

Your swaddled body, pure,
hallowed it.
Uncommon light and grace
filled every part.

I feel my heart a manger,
a feeding trough
from which the world eats
until I am empty, dry.

But if the Christ shall lie
holy, pure
inside its common shell,
filling every part,

the world of men may take
and not deplete
that ever–fresh supply
of living Bread.

SCAVENGER

The enemy, like a scavenger bird,
pecks our sin like unprotected refuse,
scatters it, litters the landscape,
then flies away in a flutter of dust
to laugh in derision and lust.

THE GIFT EXCHANGE
John 1:14, 10:29

He—God's gift to us,
wrapped in crimson pain,
in tears and sweat
and glory.
"The only Begotten—full of grace
and truth."

We—God's gift to Jesus,
wrapped in scarlet sin,
in doubt and fear
and wonder.
Chosen children, bought by love
and grace!

TRANSFIGURED

Ungainly pelican
crouched on its dry perch
broods over Tampa Bay
until some lilt of wind
or long ago memory
stirs its sluggish wings
and lifts it to pellucid clouds.
Transfigured, it soars
in sleek surrender,
gliding with gull–like grace.

And we, graceless ghosts,
huddle listlessly
on the edge of a forgotten Eden
until the breath of God
stirs spirit wings
aching with untried rhythms.
Carried on that Windward lee,
we soar unfettered,
wonder–lit and free.

When All the Candles Are Gone Away

We light our poor dark world once more
with twinkling lamps on Christmas trees,
and luminous shapes on languid lawns.
Candles on mantles and tables flicker,
and flames dance in the fireplace.
The winter moon spreads its rays,
like fingers for the diamond stars.
And we, like moths to a street lamp lured,
stumble toward the dusty light.
Warmed, renewed, recharged,
we fly, our fragile lives sustained awhile.

Poor reflections all, too weak
to warm our deep and silent cold.
Only the light of the Christ fire
rises and shines in the rigid dark
when all the candles are gone away.

Alive in Christ

She wept alone near the sepulcher, feeling as dead as He,
for in the devastated soul of her, she longed to be.
All that was noble and good, once buried there—there where she
could not bear to look—was gone. The tomb was empty.
Empty, as she so long had been, like the hollow, cast–off urn
in Simon's house where she had crouched before God's eyes should turn
and touch her heart with that holy Love for which all spirits yearn,
that love for which all shame and inconsolable secrets burn.
In that moment of truth, she came alive and gave her heart away.
Joy pranced in her soul. How could she know He wouldn't stay,
that they would hang Him on that wicked hill in the ghost–like gray
of a thousand shames and curse the universe in a single day?

Now comes the gardener through the trees. How dare he
take the Lord away, for there her anguished heart would bury
the dust of dead dreams. She would pray the world would tarry
but a moment more, when softly on the whispered air ... "Mary!"
She knew Him in an instant—like the shining of the dawn. "Rabboni!"
She knelt to embrace her hope. "Rabboni!" She should have known He
couldn't die, wouldn't die, and leave His loved ones lonely.
"I go to my Father and yours." (What bliss that He should own me
and link my name with His.) But quickly now! She must obey.
She must tell them Truth lives and banishes death away,
tell them it was Love that hanged Him in the ghost–like gray
of a thousand shames and blessed the universe in a single day!

The Trade

"Man of Sorrows" He was called,
Son of God He was.
Such a trade—a pitiful trade
and all because
of me.

A crown of thorns His gift,
a crown of glory His due.
The drops of blood—His holy blood—
because of you
rained down.

Condemned to death we were,
Restored to life instead.
"This day I pardon you, My child.
Go free," He said,
"Go free!"

Peter's Epiphany

The break of day was hardest
when the rooster mocked the morn.
It was then my soul was darkest
and my spirit three times torn.

I grieved for the ancient hills,
for breakfast by the sea
where I observed Your miracles,
Your bright divinity.

I could not comprehend
Your mission, its source.
Why couldn't power bend
and save the world by force?

But You would save it in death,
bear its shame to the cross,
forgive with Your final breath
the contemptuous, the lost.

I didn't know 'til now
when Your eyes burned into mine
that grace is the force that bows,
love the flame that refines.

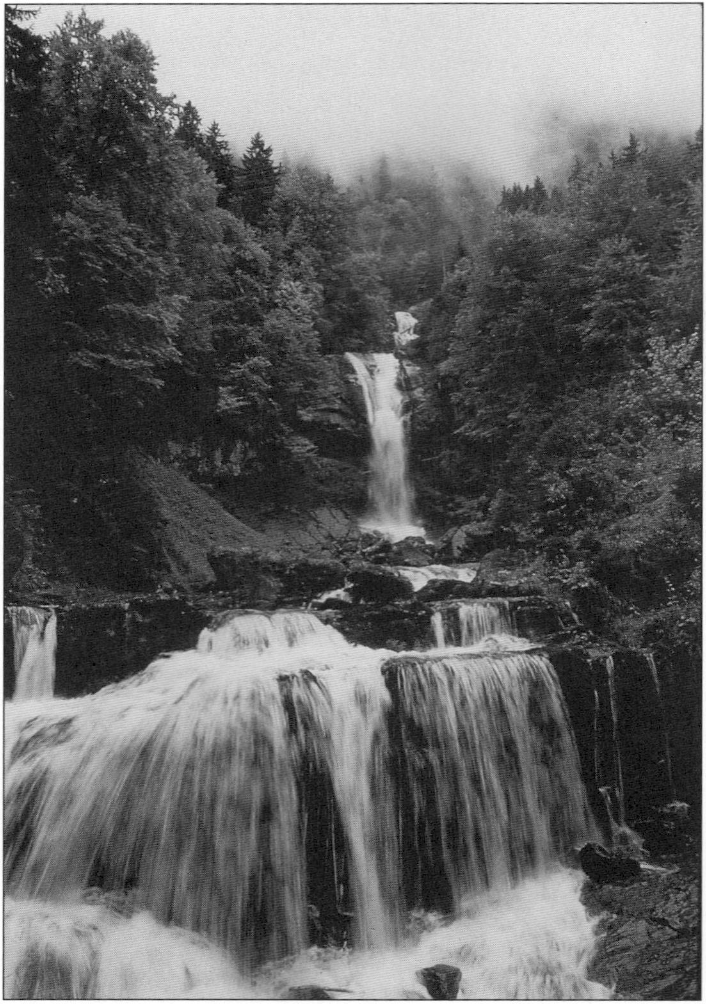

Our God Comes in the Fellowship of His Spirit

Before He was drawn away from us in a heaven–bound whirlwind, Jesus promised that we would not be left comfortless and alone. "I will not leave you as orphans; I will come to you. Before long, the world will not see Me anymore, but you will see Me. Because I live, you also will live ... peace I leave with you" (John 14:18–19, 27).

God comes ... with the energizing power of His Spirit. Our hands held fast in His, we walk the shifting, gray vales of this world until one day we walk with Him in white.

From Crisis to Cure

From brokenness to mission,
always it has been so.
Between them comes the cleansing,
the only cure for woe.

"Woe is me—a curse upon me,"
said Isaiah Ben Amos.
We need no pointing fingers.
Our own hearts quickly shame us.

Only the Savior's love
reknits the frazzled soul.
In His gaze disintegrated,
by His grace made whole.

After the Rain

Let me be a child
who with bootless feet
finds Holy Spirit puddles
to splash in.

At least let me be a passerby
who all unwitting
finds myself drenched
and dripping!

Anorexia

God is *kabod*—God is heavy!
How sits He so lightly
on His Church? On me?
Ichabod—the Church is skinny,
an insouciant scarecrow
in the dying fields of the world.

We have dieted on the world's plan
and all our strength is gone.
Do we count emaciation beauty?
Take pride in our skeletal remains?
Fatten us up, O God, with *kabod*.
Lie heavy upon us once more
'til we are filled with You.

Kabod–Hebrew for "weight"
Ichabod–Hebrew for "the weight of glory has departed"

Breathing Lessons

I need some breathing lessons.
Inhale, exhale, inhale
all that's fresh and pure
and just the right amount.
Or is there no limit
to the capacity of these lungs?
Exhale, inhale, exhale
all that is useless, spent.
Is it automatic?
No, I am breathless—straining, gasping.
My rhythm's off;
I'm dying by degrees.
Spirit, rescue me and teach me how
to live. Give me
Soul to soul
resuscitation.

The Spirit and the Church

Calls the surging, urgent Wind
howling down the passageways of grace,
scooping up lost souls like leaves
and settling them in Community.

Bold Reticence

God is holy, God is "other,"
high above our circumstance,
our little sameness. We smother
in fetid, perfumed distance
and long for Air—

the sweet, wholesome wind
of Your holy, "other" Spirit—
alive in us before we sinned,
when our ears could hear it,
hear and dare

to feel its cooling flood
through our stifling heat.
Now clothed in Blood
at Your holy feet,
we make our prayer.

Confession

O Eternal Fount,
I've been sipping Your life
through a straw
when poised like a mighty flood
You've been waiting
to pour Yourself
over me!

The Source

We think we pull from within—
our resources, our fortitude.
but it is God—
His wisdom in our absurdity,
His love in our studied neglect.

We reach for the hem of His robe,
dimly aware of Him,
but even unknowing, it is God;
it is always God
who in our frail spirits prevails.

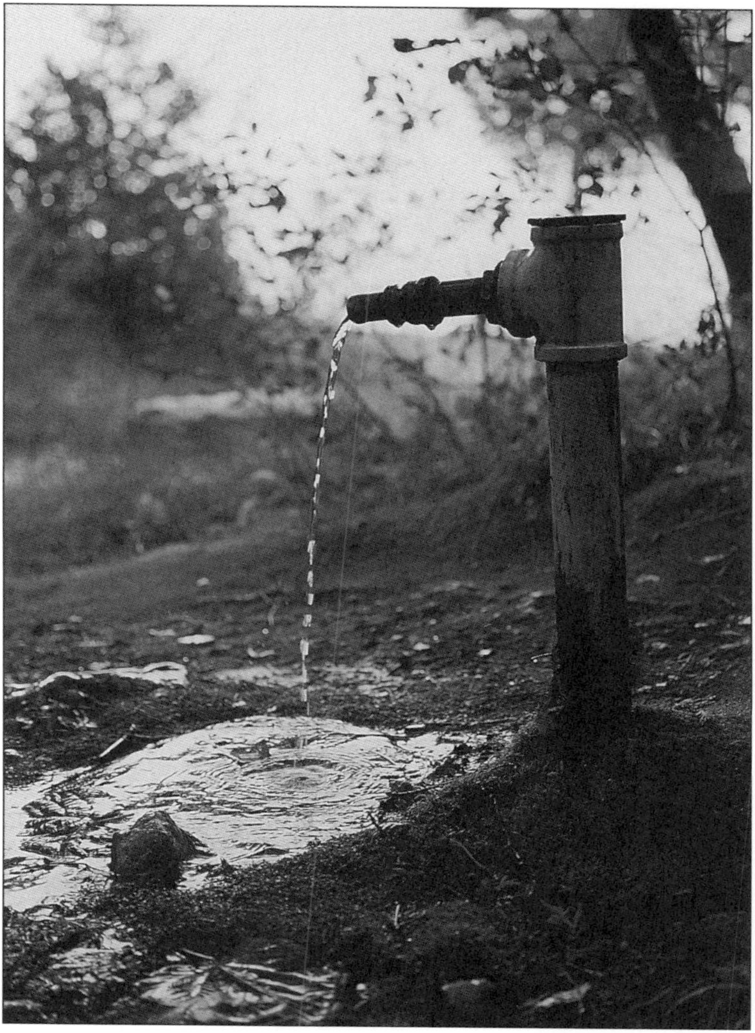

My Life Is a Poem

My life is a poem,
a searching to find
the essential image,
the central idea that
gives birth to the poem.
I strain to hear the music
inherent in the image,
to get the cadence right,
accents in the proper order.
I long to capture
words that catch the thought,
to dredge up gold in the ore.
I grasp the elusive image,
lest I lose it in the seeking
and molding and refining
and my fingers bring up nothing
but yearning for a poem.

LAODICEAN LAMENT
Revelation 2:4–5

Each candle, like a waxen ghost,
stands undetected among the host
aflame as one great burning sea
rolling toward eternity,
blending flames as a single soul,
raging, swallowing evil whole.
Who can tell which flame is lit
or which is carried in the sweep of it?
But each will one day stand alone
before the holy, pure–lit throne.
Oh, dear First Love, rekindle the flame
that burns forever to Your great Name.

INTRUSION

God's Words get in your hair,
tickle, trickle, scamper, burrow,
in your mouth—
tangy, tender, sweet, sour,
into your ears—itch, twitch.
Scratch them out, dig them out,
but desperate in their search
one slips down your throat
into your stomach but stops mid–way
and lodges in your heart.

HOSPITALITY

You usher in the flame
that kindles in the soul,
radiates and warms,
so all who enter
have respite from the cold
of self striving,
of petty hurts,
of insignificant chatter
in empty halls.
Can other souls be warmed
at this fire not really mine
but His? Oh, let the glow reach
beyond my little hearth
to the homeless at my door.

OBLATION

A crimson glow
sparkles in the cup ...
like the blood of the Holy
coursing stream and tributary,
penetrating the soul.
It cleanses, fills,
'til sated we tip our hearts
and spill the treasure
upon a thirsty world.

Proximity

A foot print, even clearly marked,
is a cold and distant thing.
Lord, I would not simply follow
but dependent, desperate, cling
to wounded hands and bleeding feet.
I long to feel Your heart
beating rhythmically and pure,
filling every part
of me. Oh, more than following,
Lord, let me cling!

Consummation

One spark,
inscrutable spark,
in the damp reaches of my soul
trembles,
caught in a whisper
of Spirit wind. Ignite the whole
furnace with flame,
cleansing flame,
til' all that's left, O Lord, is You.

Winter Meditation

Gray world,
conformed to crude design,
changed now
by snow and wind
artfully arranged.

White world
transformed like a renewed mind.
Strange how
by Spirit wind
a heart is changed.

Word Choice

These weapons are too heavy, Lord,
too fraught with terrible possibility.
Grant us please less dangerous devices!
Words burn our tongues, parch our souls,
and ricochet on a thousand fronts.
They cauterize conscience,
heal, create, delight,
or kill at close range.
Levers to lift the weak,
clubs to beat tough souls.
Remnants of refracted rhetoric
or clean lenses reflecting Light?
Why must the choice be up to us?

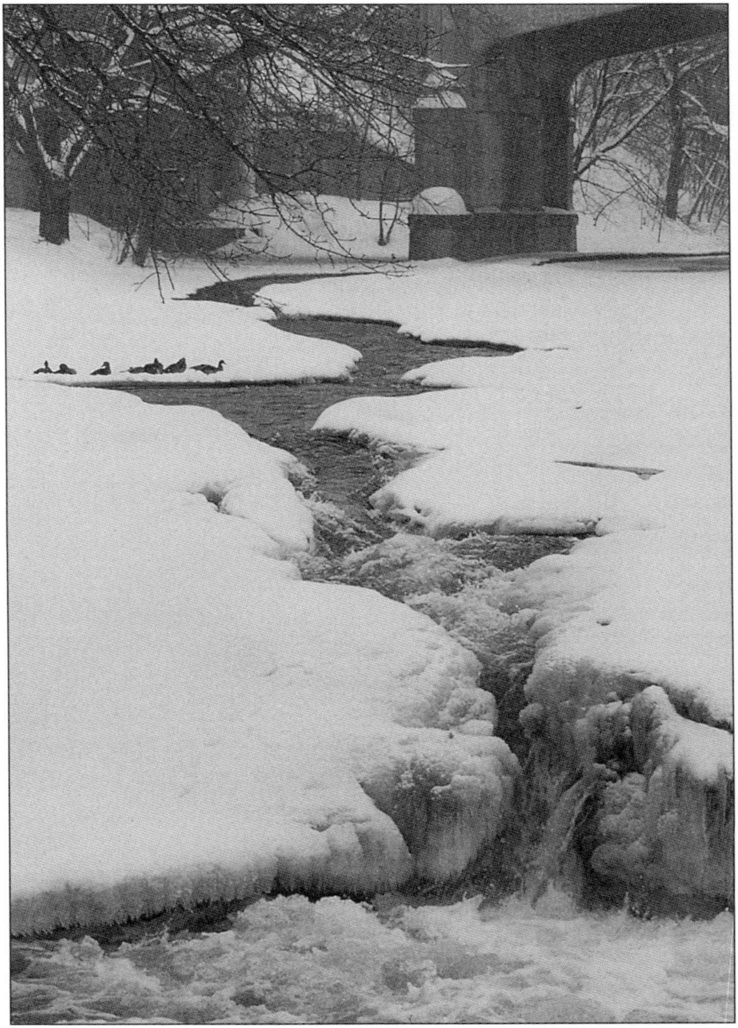

A Prayer in Wait
"For we have no power to face this vast army that is attacking us. We do not know what to do, but our eyes are upon You" (2 Chron. 20:12).

The army on the facing hill
waits in ambush, sharpens its sword
and finding its moment spills
into our peace. The frightening horde
advances, blood in their cold eyes,
but faith is in our own and flies
upward in quick and sure appeal!
We have known God's power to heal
in days gone by. And shall we now
faint before this present foe?
O, Lord, show us how
to let our quaking fears go
and when we don't know what to do
keep our eyes intent on You!

Arpeggio

Hardly prodigies—
we're novices, Lord—
unpracticed children
pledged to the Master.

We struggle with rhythm,
melody's mystic weave,
harmony's artful ardor
and the labyrinth of lyric.

Please keep marking time,
in our prayer–tuned ears,
until our noise is music
to delight Your heart!

PUNAKAIKI PUN

A surge of sea–borne wind
finds a hapless aperture
in the vulnerable rock face
and thrusts its fierceness through.
Fount through fissure erupts
in indiscriminate tears.
Anger assuaged, it melts
in anonymity
to await the next wild wave of rage.

A surge of Spirit wind
blowing through the open soul
bursts with a vigor born of love.
It sweeps heavenward, having
eased the withered soul
too long teased by surf
that only filtered back to sea
and left us petrified,
bereft, denied of all but thirst.

On seeing the blow holes in the pancake rocks at Punakaiki, New Zealand

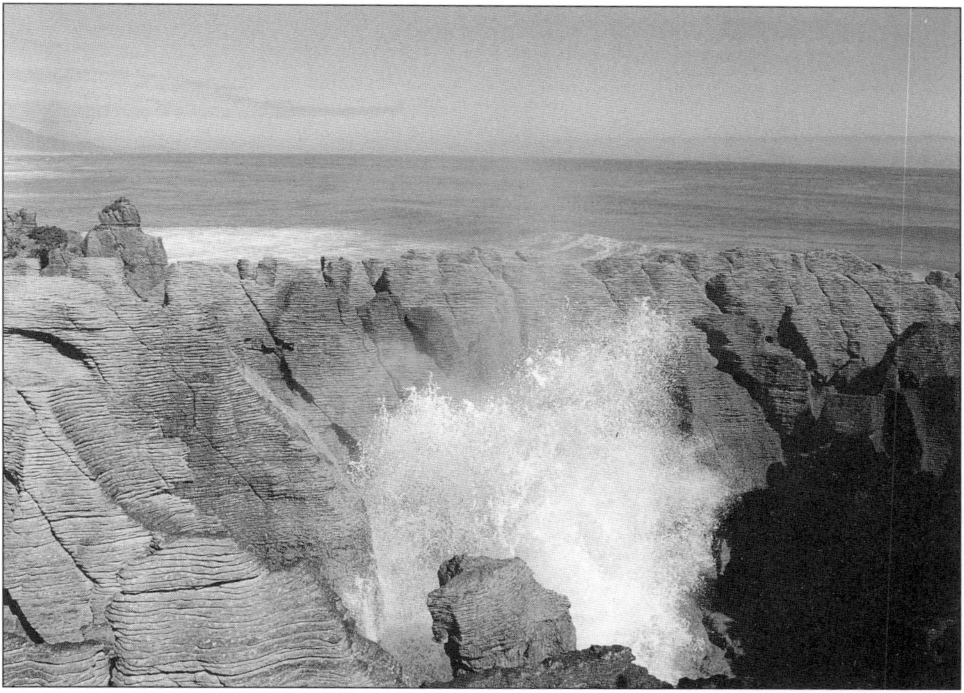

Math Problem

I have multiplied words—
page upon page
of lavished language.

But unless the Word Himself,
common Denominator of our fractured selves
total the sum of them,
my collected words
will fall empty away,
abacus beads let loose upon the world.

About the Author

Lt. Colonel Marlene Chase is editor in chief and literary secretary for Salvation Army Publications in the United States of America. She is responsible for the production of *The War Cry*, the Army's official national magazine, *Young Salvationist,* a magazine for Army youth, *Word & Deed: A Journal of Salvation Army Theology and Ministry*, and oversees a national book publishing plan under the imprint of Crest Books. She also conducts communication and publication seminars and workshops and leads journalistic tours of national and international interest.

Chase holds a bachelor of arts from Mid–America Nazarene University in Kansas City and was a delegate to the International College for Officers in London. Her writings have appeared in Army publications and Christian magazines around the world. She has written six books.

A Salvation Army officer for 35 years, Chase served 27 years in various corps and administrative appointments with her husband who was promoted to Glory in 1990. She has three children, all active in Salvation Army service, and four grandchildren.